SMALL + MODERN + URBAN =
HOME

COLLINS DESIGN

An Imprint of HarperCollinsPublishers

HarperCollins books may be purchased for educational, business, or sales promotional use.
For information, please write: Special Markets Department, HarperCollins*Publishers* Inc.,
10 East 53rd Street, New York, NY 10022.

First published in 2008 by:
Collins Design
An Imprint of HarperCollins*Publishers*
10 East 53rd Street
New York, NY 10022
Tel.: (212) 207-7000
Fax: (212) 207-7654
collinsdesign@harpercollins.com
www.harpercollins.com

Distributed throughout the world by:
HarperCollins*Publishers*
10 East 53rd Street
New York, NY 10022
Fax: (212) 207-7654

Executive editor:
Paco Asensio

Editorial coordination:
Catherine Collin

Editor:
Aitana Lleonart

Art director:
Mireia Casanovas Soley

Cover design:
Claudia Martínez Alonso

Layout:
Guillermo Pfaff Puigmartí

Library of Congress Control Number: 2008931522

ISBN: 978-0-06-154258-9

Printed in Spain

First Printing, 2008

Contents

Introduction

Changes in lifestyle in recent years have come to be reflected in our changing concept of the home, especially in cities. One of the areas where these changes have occurred with greater frequency is in the family model. It's increasingly common for people to start families later in life, making for a greater number of people who will either spend some time living alone or as a couple. Because of this, unlike in the past, when various generations lived together beneath the same roof, today's homes are shared by fewer individuals. One of the effects of this trend is that homes have gotten smaller, since demand has gone up while the number of inhabitants in each one has gone down; hence the amount of space needed has decreased as well.

These changes are also the result of many other socio-economic aspects that have forced us to question models that worked up until now. Cities continue to receive more and more people, so they must either extend their city limits or take more reasonable advantage of the space available. For one reason or another it's increasingly common to find small one or two room apartments that try to accommodate all of one's needs in a small space, in addition to offering a certain degree of comfort.

This is where architectural and interior design solutions come in, to maximize one's well-being without renouncing aesthetics. For starters, a clever distribution of space is needed to make the most of each nook and cranny while taking advantage of other elements, such as sources of light or the height of the ceiling. Given the small spaces professionals must work with in these kinds of projects, it becomes necessary to find different storage solutions. Sometimes these are provided by the architectural design itself, other times they may be achieved through the careful selection of multifunctional furniture and accessories.

The variety of projects included in this book is a perfect example of these kinds of architectural solutions which, in addition to maximizing small living quarters, manage to create unique and modern homes. You'll find everything from sober styles that rely on light and neutral shades of color for a greater sense of spaciousness, to fun and original interior designs that are full of personality and use different color palettes and a wide variety of materials. The ideas you'll find in these projects for maximizing space and gathering various functions into a single structure are practical and applicable to many types of homes. We're dealing with imaginative ideas that help to compensate for lack of space by making better use of it whether it be in lofts, apartments, duplexes or studio apartments, where the need can be even greater.

1

PLY LOFT
nARCHITECTS

■ New York, USA

▲ The spacious living room features a column rescued from the previous structure, which defines the day areas from the bedrooms.

To the left of the living room is a large work table inserted in a space formed by the plywood structure that runs around the property.

▲ The study is located in what used to be the space for the elevator, along with bookshelves that surround the desk.

One of the perimeter walls of the home is completely connected to the outdoors via a number of large windows with panel curtains. ▶

This loft unites both living quarters and work space for two artists and their families. It was decided that some of its industrial-past characteristics would be re-used in the new design. Meantime, solutions were devised for converting some of the spaces and adapting them to a new set of needs, aside from seeking out a way to visually and aesthetically unite the space at hand. For example, taking advantage of the space previously occupied by a now non-existent elevator, an office and library were built. A sinuous plywood surface was installed along one part of the loft, separating the storage areas from the other rooms, flexible enough to playfully create open areas and enclosures.

This new wooden addition surrounds and hides certain rooms, closets, columns and mechanical areas.

In complete contrast with the varied nooks and crannies created behind the plywood structure, the front of it is practically clear and open, devoid of any excess detail. This way, a sensation is achieved whereby the hallway that unites the rooms becomes more like an open and expansive area than a mere transition between one side of the apartment and the other. A wall of sliding screens placed in front of the windows serves to regulate the natural light while allowing the artists who live and work in this loft to project their video installations out onto the street.

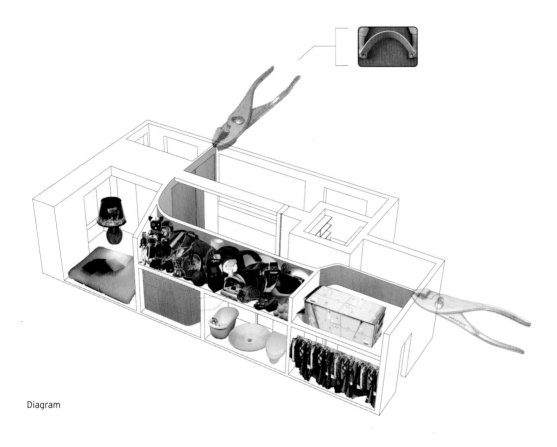

Diagram

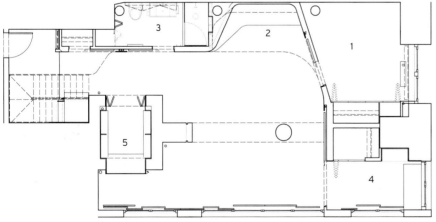

Floor plan

1. Suite
2. Desk
3. Bathroom
4. Bedroom
5. Library

The floor plan and diagram show how a flexible plywood surface runs around the loft and changes some straight angles
into curves which conceal a number of rooms.

The ample ceiling height allows for a second level to be created expressly for the bed in the children's bedroom. ▲

▲ A visual mix of modern elements with others that came with
the original space can be found in the main bedroom.

The bathroom is behind a sliding door in the entry to the loft. ▶
Its straight and simple lines are highlighted by the use of
white, with brown details.

2

INTERLOCKING PUZZLE LOFT
Kyu Sung Woo Architects

■ New York, USA

▲ The large window illuminates both floors of the apartment. The white walls and light-colored timber reflect the light more intensely.

The breakfast bar can be extended to form an L-shape in the ▶ living room to convert into the dining room table, around which a number of stools have been placed.

▲ Big, tall pieces of furniture were eliminated from the living room to emphasize the height of the ceiling and the feeling of space.

The kitchen is framed by the structure that forms the upper ▶ level. The fridge is embedded in the wall, with the cupboards opposite.

This loft's vaulted ceiling impeded the comfortable installation of the two complete floors required to make this home a true duplex. For this reason, a series of interlaced and assembled volumes were designed to help take most advantage of actual space, creating a second level only in certain areas. The loft's full height is reserved for the dining room and living room, allowing full advantage to be taken of the natural light coming in through the tall, wide windows. A second level was built on the other side of the apartment. A staircase leads to the upper level, where two bedrooms are located. These are suspended above a structure that houses the closets, taking advantage of the space below. A catwalk grants access to the bedrooms above the kitchen, which form a rectangle that is almost fully enclosed thanks to the structural shape of the closets. This visual effect is achieved by the continuity of the countertop, which creates a small bar that serves as a dining room table.

The color palette used was determined by the number of materials used. All of the horizontal surfaces and the catwalk to the bedrooms are covered with maple wood; all the remaining vertical surfaces, as well as the ceiling, have been painted white. Glass separates the bedroom from the living room beside it, thus avoiding the loss of any natural light to the room.

Section

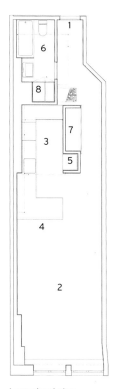

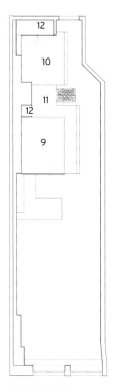

Lower level plan

Upper level plan

1. Entrance
2. Living room
3. Kitchen
4. Dining area
5. Refrig. alcove
6. Bathroom
7. Closet
8. Storage
9. Sleeping platform A
10. Sleeping platform B
11. Catwalk
12. Closet

The kitchen stands below the platform that holds the bed- ▲
rooms and behind the structure that hides the closet.

◄ The structure that forms the top floor, where the bedroom is located, is in turn used as a closet below, on the other side of the kitchen.

To access the upper level, where the two bedrooms are, a ▲ stairway was constructed in the hollow space.

◀ The corridor that runs to the foot of the bed has been covered in maple wood to make the bedroom look warmer.

The living room can be seen from one of the bedrooms, ▲ thus enjoying the natural light passing through the glass.

3

FLORENCE RESIDENCE
The Lawrence Group Architects

■ New York, USA

▲ The painting on the brick wall behind the sofa has a detail in the same light blue color that is repeated throughout the apartment.

The living room, where a wall covered in plant-motif paper ▶ presides, provides access to the bedroom, protected behind the bookshelves that form the library.

◀ The dining room table, crowned by a magnificent chandelier, is unusually high, which is why timber and forged-iron stools have been used instead of chairs.

The kitchen has been used as a set for a number of cooking ▶ shows and photographic sessions and is located against a varnished brick wall.

This project is the result of converting a traditional apartment into a loft to live and work in. The conventional rooms, like the living room, dining room, kitchen and bedrooms, are combined into one space where day to day activities co-exist together. Aside from its residential uses, this apartment has another added function. It also serves as a television set for taping the cooking show *Tyler's Ultimate*, and is a photo studio for cookbooks and similar projects. Because of this, a comfortable loft was designed that at the same time presented a different and innovative style as special background for its second function. The interplay of different textures and materials provides a lot of personality. For the kitchen, a wall of varnished brick separates this room from the dining area. The living room boasts an impressive wallpaper of vegetation-inspired designs on a black background. Materials like wood and the use of browner tones, beige and earthen colors creates a set of elements, inspired by nature, that contrast with other elements, like the large chandelier or the stainless steel kitchen furniture. The color blue appears in subtle brush-strokes throughout the apartment, including in the mural hanging on the bare brick wall behind the sofa. The bedroom is separated by a translucent wall which doubles as a bookcase on the side facing the living room.

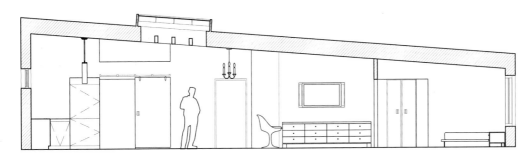

Section

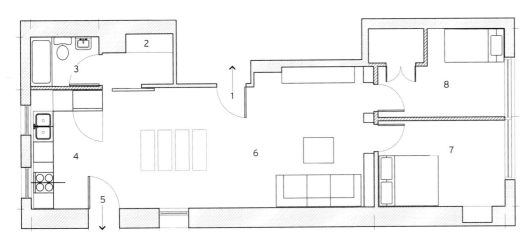

Floor plan

1. Entrance
2. Storage
3. Bathroom
4. Kitchen
5. To deck
6. Living room
7. Master bedroom
8. Bedroom

◀ This plan shows how only the bedrooms and the bathroom are separated from the other areas, which form a single space.

The apartment's long shape and the lack of walls result in an ▲ overall view of the entire apartment from any side.

14

APARTMENT H
Gavin Harris, Henrietta Reed/Mackay & Partners

■ London, UK

▲ Mirrors completely cover one wall of the apartment, from the living room to the bedroom. This makes it seem bigger.

The bathroom is opposite the kitchen, hidden behind the mir- ▶ rors which also mostly conceal the cupboards.

◢ A small space free of cupboards was left in the mirrored wall and a little study positioned there, in front of the entrance hall.

The practical dining room table, on which an image has been ▶ engraved in bright pink, is extracted from the living room sideboard. The dining room table is hidden in the sideboard and only brought out when needed. This provides another solution to the problem of space.

The existence of only two windows, one on each side of the apartment, provoked the need to take full advantage of these two natural light sources. A simple color palette was chosen, mostly white, along with smooth and reflective surfaces. The ceiling and walls were finished in polished plaster, achieving a neutral ensemble marked by the occasional appearance of vibrant colors and textures. Since the apartment belonged to a couple with no children, the division of space was relatively simple: a private area for the bedroom on one side, and the rest of the rooms divided throughout the other side. Despite this, a complete view of the space can be had from the hall in the middle of the apartment. To unite the space, a series of enormous, floor-to-ceiling mirrors were installed along one of the walls. This way, the light that comes in from the two windows is reflected throughout the space, lending it a greater sense of spaciousness. These mirrors hide a wardrobe closet in the bedroom, a desk beside the hall and provide an entertainment space in the lounge, while offering ample storage space as well. In the living room, a system has been arranged that hides the dining room table inside the sideboard, from which it can be easily pulled. Also hidden behind the mirrored wall is the bathroom, where pearled white tile covers the floors, ceiling and walls. A floral mosaic along one of the bathroom walls lends a touch of color.

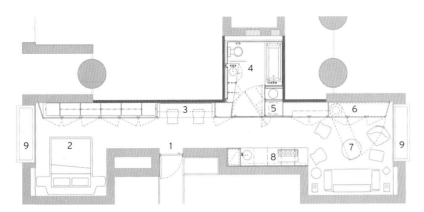

Floor plan

1. Entry
2. Bedroom
3. Study
4. Bathroom
5. Laundry
6. Dining unit
7. Lounge
8. Kitchen
9. Planters

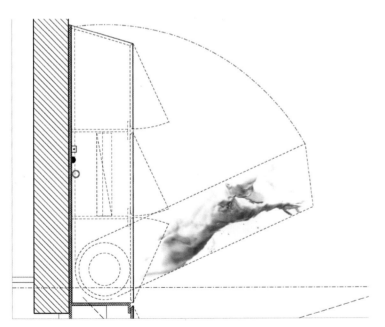

Table top

◀ This plan shows the mechanism that lets you pull the dining table top out from the living room sideboard thanks to a shaft located at one end.

The floral mosaic covering one of the bathroom walls lends ▲ color while contrasting with the purer lines of the furniture.

◀ This apartment has two entries of light: one window in the
living room and another exactly opposite, in the bedroom.

The mirrored wall running along one side of the apartment ▲
ends in the bedroom, where it hides the dressing room.

5

APARTMENT IN PARIS
Flora de Gastines & Anne Geistdoerfer/Double G

■ Paris, France

Photos: © André Thoraval

▲ The apartment is flush against the ground floor. It is accessed from a small garden. The colors of the plants and flowers are repeated in the apartment's décor.

Various design pieces stand out in this project, such as the ▶ black stool by Bishop of India Mahdavi and the rocking chair, a modern design classic from Charles and Ray Eames.

40

▲ The sculptural spiral staircase next to the living room connects the two levels and is visually integrated by being white like the walls.

The electrical household appliances and kitchenware are hidden inside the cupboards so they are not all out on display, as the kitchen shares the same space as the living room. ▶

This small 484 square-foot space consists of one ground level and an attic, both areas covered by stained glass windows. The façade of the home reveals bare brickwork, with translucent glass and green-painted carpentry that mixes with the patio vegetation. This small studio space is given a greater sense of spaciousness by way of white walls that contrast sharply with the black stone-tiled floor. The furniture, lamps and accessories add touches of color. On the lower level are the kitchen, dining room and a bathroom. The bedroom and dressing room are in the attic, which is reached by means of a spiral staircase beside the living room that practically seems like a sculpture in itself. The metal staircase and upper catwalk have been lacquered white to lessen the space's industrial aspect.

The kitchen opens up into the living room. Its appliances and kitchenware are hidden in the white furniture, which has been given a Corian countertop and a sink finished in orange resin. In the living room, the white Flexform sofa faces a huge cotton mattress with orange felt cushions. The contemporary design furniture, like the Charles and Ray Eames chair, the Big Swing lamp and the Bishop of India Mahdavi stool create a relaxing little corner with a lot of personality. On the upper floor, the curtain that hides the dressing area can be closed to hide the bedroom and prevent light from coming in.

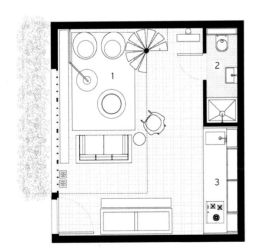

Lower level floor plan

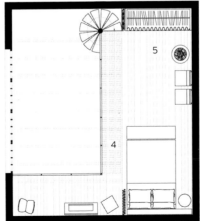

Upper level floor plan

1. Living room
2. Bathroom
3. Kitchen
4. Bedroom
5. Dressing area

◀ The bathroom is next to the kitchen, just below the dressing area on the upper floor.

In order to make it a more pleasant place, the appliances and ▲ kitchen tools are hidden inside the kitchen furniture.

▲ A small library has been placed beside the bedroom, along with an original green Flora lamp by Marie Christophe.

Closing the curtains on the top floor visually protects the ▶ bedroom and dressing area from the floor below.

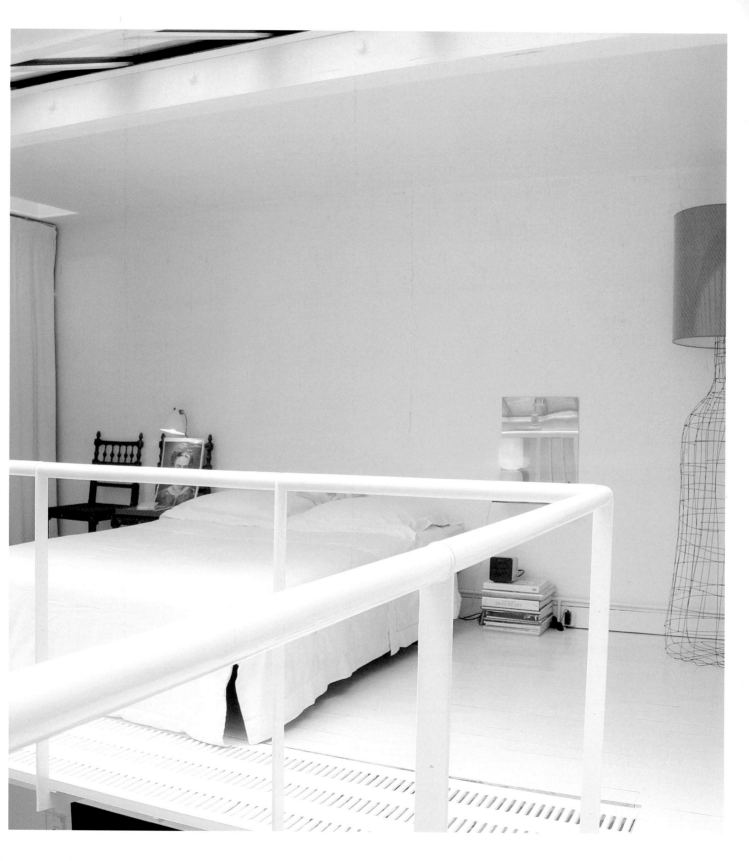

6

DUPLEX IN BRUSSELS

Bruno Vanbesien

■ Brussels, Belgium

Photos: © Hendikx Diane/Owi.bz

▲ The large windows in the living room make it possible to illuminate both floors, as the two levels of the duplex are visually united.

Neutral colors like black and white, as well as timber tones, ▶ make the red wall against the staircase really stand out.

▲ To integrate the kitchen spaces as much as possible, an island was built that can be passed on either side to reach the terrace.

The wall opposite the kitchen is coated in slate. Behind it is a ▶ small guest bathroom.

This duplex forms part of a remodeling project of a house in Brussels from the first half of the 19th century. The building underwent various changes over time, some of which contributed to it losing most of its original features. The architect decided to gut the property completely and design four units, one of which is this duplex.

Because the size of the property was reduced to less than 1,000 square feet, the main aim was to make it look as spacious as possible without renouncing functionality. By getting rid of part of the first floor area, the ceiling is twice as high in the living room. This ensures a lot more natural light and that the two floors remain connected. The whole property has been laid with the same parquet flooring, including the bath-room and kitchen, in a tone similar to that of the beams. This means the different functions flow from one space to another and achieve a much roomier appearance.

To reach the upper floor, a discreet staircase in projecting steel was built against the red wall of the living room. This floor includes the office, bedroom and another bathroom. The areas are separated by various sliding panels which replace immobile walls and make it possible to distribute the space in different ways, according to need. The timber-toned floor and beams have been combined with a palette of three basic colors: red, white and black, repeated throughout the project, as well as green in the bathroom.

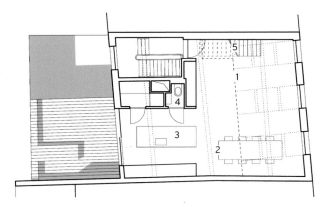

Lower floor plan

1. Living room
2. Dining room
3. Kitchen
4. Bathroom
5. Stairs
6. Study
7. Bedroom

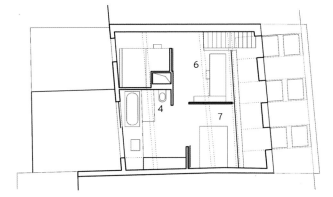

Upper floor plan

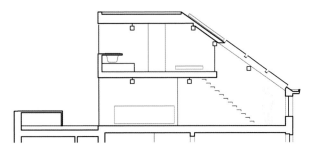

Section

◀ This section shows how height was used upstairs, which at its lowest point protrudes over the ground-floor living room.

At the end of the kitchen is the balcony with timber decking, ▲ making it a great entry of light for the lower level.

◄ The property is so small that the stairway was designed with projecting stairs so the space beneath it could be used.

The inclined window is one of the main entries of light in the ► small study located above the living room.

The wood flooring provides access to the bathtub, below the ▶
window. In this case, the color green makes for a calm and
relaxing space.

7

LA ROSSA
PTang Studio

■ Hong Kong, China

Photos: © Ulso Tsang

▲ A large mural reproducing trees and branches in different tones of brown is featured on one wall of the living area.

The color red is present in every room and each element of ▶ this apartment, such as the dining room chairs, the rug, the sideboard and the cushions in the living room.

▲ The sophisticated and romantic look of the property comes from details such as the grand chandelier hanging above the dining room table.

A red flower, the reflection of a pattern that decorates the ▶ glass of the office, can be seen in the corridor. It defines the space and avoids the need for opaque partitions.

In determining this apartment's design, a premise was established upon which to base it: a styling based on the color red being superimposed over the purity of a white background. With this, an energetic and lively combination could be achieved while remaining feminine and romantic in certain areas. The drawings and floral prints are reiterated in each of the rooms, covering either entire walls or the glass partitions. In the living/dining room located at the very entrance, the low television table extends out as if it were but one more rug. This table stands out with a red lacquered finish that contrasts well with the mural of a bunch of tree branches that covers one of the walls. Glamour and sophistication appear by way of the majestic glass chandelier that hangs suspended above the dining room table and gives this corner of the apartment personality.

The office, located at the beginning of the hallway that marks the path to the private rooms, is separated by a glass wall adorned by large red flowers that contrast with the intensely gray walls. This color change helps separate the space visually without having to resort to the kind of unnecessary enclosures that the glass wall replaces. In this small corner they needed another allusion to nature, which was resolved by a tree shaped bookcase. The rooms display a wallpaper faithful to the apartment's color scheme, though they incorporate beige and brown tones. In the main bedroom, the wall, bed and closet are covered with floral prints and embroidery.

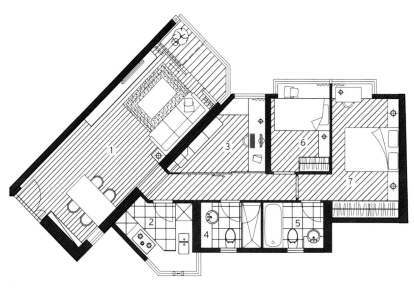

Floor plan

1. Living and dining room
2. Kitchen
3. Studio
4. Bathroom
5. Bathroom
6. Bedroom
7. Master bedroom

◀ The dining room is reached from the entrance and shares the same space as the living room, located on the other side of the door that leads to the other rooms.

In order to avoid enclosures and achieve a larger visual unity, one of the office's sides is made of glass. ▲

▲ Stripes completely decorate the bedroom walls and increase the intensity of the colors on the side with the headboard.

The floral motifs are reiterated in the bedrooms, though in a ▶ much more subtle and elegant way.

8

PIER 24 COPENHAGEN
Kim Utzon Arkitekter

■ Islands Brygge, Copenhagen, Denmark

Photos: © Carlos Cezanne

▲ The neutrality of the property's basic tones made it possible to reserve the bright colors for the living room furniture.

This property has two big entries of light, one in the living ▶ room and the other in the kitchen. Large glass windows were installed to make the most of it.

▲ The lack of furniture and decorative elements forms part of the style and personality of this apartment.

In the living room, in front of a traditional closet, are the sofa ▶ and the bright coffee tables lacquered in different tones of red and orange.

This 851 square-foot apartment gains size and space thanks to the sparse amount of furniture. The majority of the pieces are placed at a distance from the walls, leaving the perimeter practically free of elements and achieving a greater sense of spaciousness. In addition, these walls are painted completely white. The neutrality of this color, together with the light-colored parquet wood and the apartment's abundant natural light, permitted the use of daring and brightly-colored furniture in the living room. The serious and elegant dark leather sofa provides a counterpoint to the red and orange lacquered tables in the middle and the original armchair with three holes. Behind it, a large painting placed directly on the floor gives the space a very personal feeling despite the apartment's naked appearance. The same pattern is repeated in the kitchen, respecting the white colors and light browns that combine well with the also earth-toned sink. Just beyond the kitchen is the dining room, with its simple wood-plank table on trestles and Charles and Ray Eames-designed Eames Plastic chairs surrounding it. Small notes of color are also present in this area, whether it is the fruit bowl on the table or the VIPP wastepaper baskets. Simplicity is also sought in the bedroom and the bathroom by recurring neutral tones. One of the elements that characterize this project is the placement of paintings in every room. These are usually leaning against the wall, giving the project an unfinished air and a strong art-gallery appearance.

◀ The dining room table is made from a wooden board supported on two trestles. It is surrounded by seats designed by the Eames brothers.

Designer furniture gives the dining room its personality and ▲ a discreet, dark-colored painting decorates the wall.

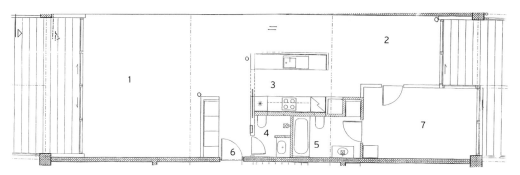

Floor plan

1. Living room
2. Dining room
3. Kitchen
4. Bathroom 1
5. Bathroom 2
6. Entrance
7. Bedroom

◄ In the bedroom, the decorative elements have been placed directly onto the parquet floor.

The VIPP kitchen trash bin stands out against the white ▲ tones and light-colored timber repeated throughout the apartment.

9

SMALL SPACE
Poponcini & Lootens Architecten

■ Antwerp, Belgium

Photos: © Sarah Blee/Owi.bz

▲ The studio is the first space you reach from the entrance and is perfectly illuminated on both sides thanks to the large windows.

At the far end of the studio is a courtyard that enables a window onto the outside, which illuminates and ventilates the space. ▶

▲ The kitchen is protected within a black cube, which in turn subtly divides the rest of the property, creating one zone for the living room and another for the dining area.

The dining area is visually linked with the kitchen via a rectangular window open at one end of the structure. ▶

The entrance of this house opens directly onto the studio of the owners, both landscape architects. This in turn leads to a small inside courtyard. One of the walls of the courtyard was kept in its original state in tribute to the old construction. Elements such as stone, small fir trees and plants make it an oasis of nature in the middle of the city. The main floor of the house is reached via solid metal stairs and includes the main daytime areas, such as the kitchen, dining room and living room, which share the same space.

The kitchen was designed inside a black cube on the open-plan first floor, opposite another exit to a balcony with a metal-mesh floor which enables you to look down onto the courtyard below. The cube was given a small window that connects the kitchen with the space used as the dining area, which protects the living room behind it. The metal stairs lead to another floor, with two small bedrooms for the children. The narrow corridor that leads to the children's rooms conceals a small bathroom behind sliding doors. Finally, the main bedroom is on the top floor and contains a bathroom. This room has large floor-to-ceiling windows and a sliding glass door that opens onto the balcony. The flooring is an element that differentiates the home from the studio, as the floors used for the home are laid with parquet and add the feeling of warmth that wood provides.

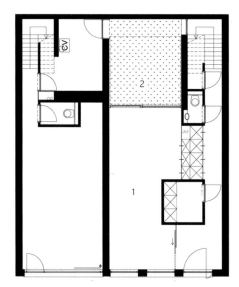

Ground floor plan

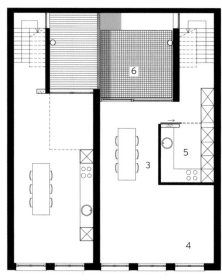

First floor plan

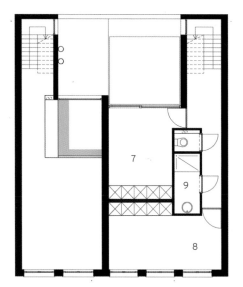

Second floor plan

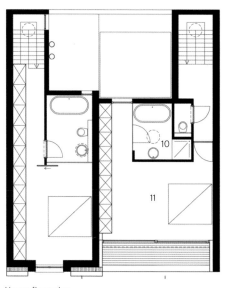

Upper floor plan

1. Studio
2. Courtyard
3. Dining room
4. Living room
5. Kitchen
6. Terrace
7. Bedroom 1
8. Bedroom 2
9. Bathroom 1
10. Bathroom 2
11. Master bedroom

The kitchen cupboards feature yellow translucent glass slid- ▲
ing doors. One bench doubles up as the breakfast bar.

▲ The solid and robust metal staircase contrasts with the white walls between which it is framed.

Big, bright plant pots decorate the first floor balcony, where ▶ the metal-mesh floor makes it possible to observe the courtyard below.

▲ The two children's rooms are on the same floor, one at either end of the corridor and separated by the bathroom.

The sliding doors in the corridor conceal two rooms, a small ▶ one for the toilet and a larger one for the rest of the bath-room.

10

WEST 87TH STREET APARTMENT

Leone Design Studio

■ New York, USA

Photos: © Mikiko Kikuyama

▲ The birch plywood that covers the kitchen table is also used on the wall and ceiling, creating a visual separation with respect to the other spaces.

The living and dining areas share the same space as the ▶ kitchen. The bathroom is behind the yellow kitchen wall.

▲ A series of decorated large windows runs along one side of the apartment through to the bedroom.

The bedroom has been positioned in a fairly narrow space ▶ but has a spacious dressing area right behind it, reached via the living/dining room.

This small apartment required a complete makeover due to its state of deterioration. With the new design, the architects attempt to maximize useful space while lending it a spacious atmosphere. The space occupied by the bathroom and kitchen was completely redesigned and adapted to fit another piece of kitchen furniture that serves as a new countertop with more drawers and cabinets for storage. This new structure stretches into the dining room, where it becomes a sideboard beside the table. Its plywood top is also used on part of the dining room wall, where it stretches all the way to the ceiling and has the effect of enclosing this area within the kitchen's limits. In this fashion, a visual separation is achieved between this little area and the rest of the space, while an aesthetic continuity is created by the tone of the parquet used for the floor.

The only room in the apartment was divided into two different spaces: one for the dressing room and one for the bedroom. The result is a maximized space for storage furniture and wardrobe that also lends much more privacy to the rest area. In the small bathroom, the white color of the floor tiles and shelves predominates while combining with the sink's dark wood.

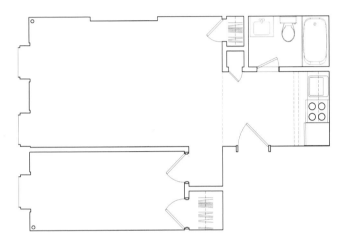

Existing floor plan

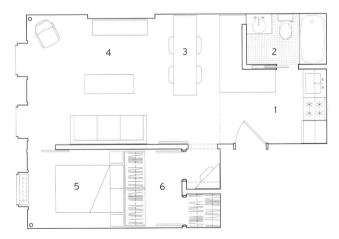

New floor plan

1. Kitchen
2. Bathroom
3. Dining room
4. Living room
5. Bedroom
6. Dressing room

The floor of the old bedroom created a division of this ▲
space, allowing the design of a separate dressing room.

11

DUPLEX IN DRUFAYSTRAAT

Dick van Gameren Architecten

■ Amsterdam, Netherlands

Photos: © Luuk Kramer

▲ From the outside we can see the large window that used to be the store front before the property was converted into a home.

The large window means the basement areas also enjoy light ▶ and have a good view outdoors.

▲ The stairs that can lead either to the lower floor or the first floor are right inside the entrance. You can see the corner with the dining room as you descend the stairs.

Next to the dining room, in the same open space, is the ▶ kitchen, with a long worktop on one side and the stove and oven opposite.

Prior to becoming a duplex apartment, this location in the Amsterdam neighborhood of Oud-Zuid had been a clothing store. This explains the huge window beside the door; at one time it was a shop window. The triangular floor plan results from the building's location at the very corner of a residential block. The space had been a street-level store with a backroom and another one off to the side, each elevated about three feet off the ground.

When the new owner obtained the location, the floor of the store had been removed, leaving only the additional rooms and a wide-open view of the basement. It was decided that in order to take full advantage of the space a duplex would be created. The basement was kept and a new floor was built level with the two rooms that remained above. By making the entire floor match this three-foot elevation, a greater intimacy was achieved without having to cover the shop's window, which serves as one large light source. Consequently, set just beside the duplex's main entrance, two staircases were installed to allow access to the top floor or the floor below. The bottom level houses the kitchen and dining room, located precisely beneath the shop window. It also has an additional room and a bathroom. The top floor is slightly distanced from the window and, sheltered behind a wooden, balcony-like structure, we find a well-lit work area. The back room now serves as the living room while the old side room now doubles as a toy room for the kids.

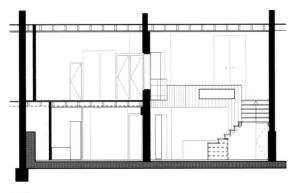
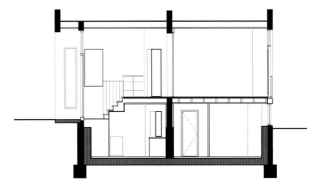

Sections

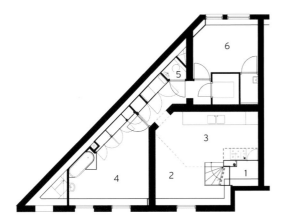

Lower level plan

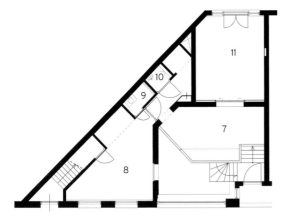

Upper level plan

1. Hall
2. Dining room
3. Kitchen
4. Master bedroom
5. Bathroom 1
6. Bedroom
7. Studio
8. Playroom
9. Bathroom 2
10. Bathroom 3
11. Living room

The distance between the floor and the window creates inti- ▲
macy without losing light from the huge front window.

◀ A basic material used in the duplex is wood, lending warmth while adding to the purity of the white colors.

Two large windows preside over the room located on the first ▲ floor, with parquet flooring and timber-covered walls.

▲ The main bedroom, located in the basement, was provided with two skylights to allow contact with the exterior.

The washbasin and bathtub are also located in the main bedroom, sharing the same space. ▶

12

METROPOLITAN CHIC
Mohen Design International

■ Shanghai, China

▲ White is the most characteristic element of this property, which has a luxurious and sophisticated look.

The dining room features a brown rug that adds a splash of ▶ color. Beneath the sideboard, flush with the floor and inserted in the empty space, is an original shelf.

▲ A large mirror was positioned on one wall of the entrance, behind which is a closet for keeping umbrellas and keys.

The dining room table is inserted in an empty space between ▶ the kitchen and one of the bedrooms, next to an outdoor entrance the curtains conceal.

This project was a true challenge for its designers, who had to think up a way of designing a common area that could include a living room and dining room, a kitchen, two rooms and a bathroom; all without renouncing careful design and open spaces while working within the confines of a 795 square-foot space. Each area is clearly separated. The vestibule divides the space into two sides. This way, the living room faces the kitchen and dining room, which are located on the other side of this imaginary line. On the other side, the main room faces the guest bedroom, or the study, considering that the room can be converted for either purpose. Decorative excess has been pushed aside in favor of naked walls or, in the vestibule's case, completely covered by a mirror behind which is a place to put shoes, umbrellas or house keys. The frequent use of these resources, mirrors and transparent or reflective materials, makes the apartment seem bigger.

The details of the ceiling, which is segmented by grooves, much like the carefully chosen placement of the hanging lamps, are elements that subtly divide the areas and give each of them their own space. Yellow and light brown are repeated throughout the apartment to create a warm atmosphere characterized by a personal and simple luxury.

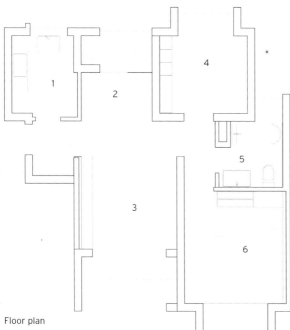

Floor plan

1. Kitchen
2. Dining room
3. Living room
4. Bedroom
5. Bathroom
6. Bedroom

◄ Although the living and dining rooms are visually united, the space is clearly differentiated by being separated by the corridor that leads to the bathroom and the bedrooms.

The use of mirrors and translucent materials lends a greater ▲ sense of spaciousness to the main bedroom.

13

IT'S FAB TO HAVE MY OWN PAD

Pablo Fernández Lorenzo & Pablo Redondo Díez

■ Madrid, Spain

Photos: © Pablo Fernández Lorenzo

▲ White adds depth and space to this L-shaped loft. It enables natural light to reverberate and be used to full advantage.

The glass-encased shower joins the kitchen and forms a ► large island which runs along the narrow corridor that unites the bedroom with the living/dining room.

▲ Cupboards have been fitted in one wall of the corridor and the toilet has been concealed. When the toilet door is open it joins the shower and separates the private areas from the rest of the loft.

This picture shows the doors behind which the toilet is joined ▶ with the shower. On the other side, another sliding door can be closed to isolate the bathroom completely.

It is becoming more common for some people to decide to live alone. Because of this choice, they expect to enjoy every inch of space in their home at any given moment while attempting to avoid unnecessary walls, doors and partitions. This 753 square-foot apartment has an L-shaped layout stretched between two points of light: the light coming from the street on one side and the light coming from the interior patio on the other. The idea was to leave the space as open as possible in order to allow for a wider view of the whole. The first move was to install a divided bathroom where the shower and the sink occupy a central position in the living quarters, completely surrounded by transparent glass. In front of these is the toilet, enclosed in a closet with two doors that, when opened, perfectly align with the glass around the shower and sink; thus creating a complete bathroom that keeps in sounds and odors. A sliding door and a curtain, affixed to the glass with magnets, allow for visual separation from the rest of the apartment when entertaining guests.

In this fashion, the alterations were based on two concepts: extend the wall to create a 46 foot-long strip of closet space capable of storing everything, including part of the bathroom; and install a 14 foot, stainless steel table that comprises the open kitchen and is capable of being covered, considering that the white worktop is retractable. On the other side of the L, the dining room, living room and studio may be found, all sharing the same space.

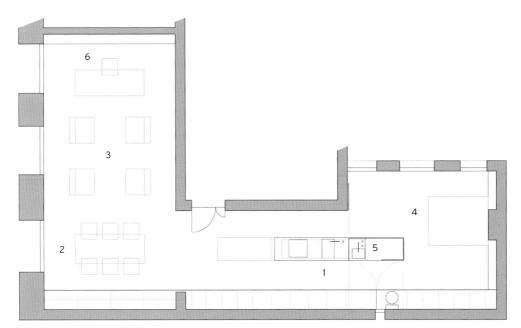

Floor plan

1. Kitchen
2. Dining room
3. Living room
4. Bedroom
5. Bathroom
6. Studio

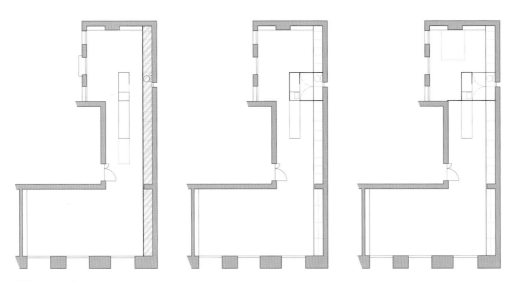

Bathroom enclosure

◀ These plans show the different types of partition walls that make it possible to unite the toilet with the shower and wash-basin or isolate it from the rest of the apartment if required.

The doors hiding part of the bathroom can open up against ▲ the shower and sink, separating it from the rest of the loft.

◄ On the kitchen's other side, the loft widens into an open space where the dining room, living room and study are located.

The surface is a polyurethane finished epoxy, while the car- ▲ pentry is made of DM with a lacquered white matte finish.

The bedroom is on the other side of the dining room, next to ▶
the glass cube that separates the shower and continues the
idea of the kitchen island.

14

CHEN RESIDENCE
CJ Studio

■ Hsindzu, Taiwan

Photos: © CJ Studio

▲ The different zones of the house have been distributed to make use of the two levels the platform creates. For example, the living room is positioned in one of the empty spaces formed.

The kitchen is sheltered behind the living room and camou- ▶ flaged between the white walls. It features a small breakfast bar with stools.

▲ One of the most unusual features of this project is the structure that separates the daytime areas from the private zones and which forms a spacious cupboard on either side.

A translucent glass sliding door was used to keep the office ▶ private, without having to use more separation elements.

This project suggests a layout based on spatial continuity through a floor plan that unites every room while maintaining the specific function of each one. To achieve this, some very different and original resources were used. One of these is based on the floor's different levels, which visually separate the areas. These also provide transitional elements between one space and another by means of a catwalk. Another creative resource in the architect's design of this apartment is the construction of an unfinished, curved wall. Situated right in the middle, it serves to visually separate the more private areas, like the bedroom, bathroom and office, from the hall, the living room and the kitchen.

This large structure serves as an element of distribution, while offering ample storage space in the living room. On the other side it serves as a bedroom closet that is separated from the office by a paneled structure that, once closed, becomes a large mirror. Just on the other side of the bedroom is the bathroom, raised on one of the levels in the floor that are repeated throughout the project. The numerous windows that run along two sides of the apartment allow for a lot of light, an element kept in mind when decorating the apartment. Light tones of white, earth and wood were chosen for all the surface areas. The simplicity of the furniture allows the apartment's structures and interior architecture to stand out.

Floor plan

1. Entrance
2. Office
3. Bedroom
4. Bathroom
5. Living room
6. Kitchen

◀ The shape of the table emulates the structure and perimeter of the office; it becomes wider on the more spacious side, next to the window.

Closing the paneled door completely achieves intimacy in ▲ the bedroom. Once extended, it doubles as a mirror.

The large structure visually separating the private area ▲
from the rest of the loft is also a bedroom closet.

◀ The bathroom is beside the room, raised on one of the plat-
forms that subtly delineate the different areas.

Pure, simple lines and materials like glass were used in the ▲
bathroom, particularly for the shower and washbasin.
Opaque elements were used as sparingly as possible.

PIAZZA BIANCAMANO APARTMENT

DAP Studio

■ Milan, Italy

Photos: © Andrea Martiradonna

▲ The structure that composes the kitchen, next to the entrance to the apartment, is the main element in this project. It subtly separates and distributes the different zones.

The dining and living rooms are located in front of the ▶ kitchen and share the same space, while the bedroom and bathroom are concealed behind.

▲ The corridor formed by the kitchen and the wall with the cupboards provides access to the private area, protected behind the modular element behind the sofa.

The privileged location of this home on the fourteenth floor of a building planted in the center of Milan drove the architects to take best advantage of its warm light and its connection with the exterior. A view of the city may be enjoyed from any point in the apartment. The floor plan arises from a desire to avoid enclosures, achieving instead an open space for fluid circulation. These same functional elements create a certain space distribution that differentiates each area without sacrificing any perception of the whole. Distinction between day areas and night areas is not exactly clear; the place is laid out in a gradual manner, ever more intimate, until finally reaching the bedroom. The kitchen island, a structure which connects with the ceiling and houses cabinets on its other side, is open towards the dining/living room while providing behind itself a hallway that leads to the more private areas. Another example of the continuity between the apartment's different areas is the wall behind the sofa, with openings on either side that won't impede traffic while still hiding the bedroom. Straight lines, the juxtaposition of areas, and surfaces of different degrees of transparency are what create this apartment's landscape, which is paved with polished stone. Paint and white enamel were chosen for the walls, while the furniture sports white, lacquered wood and Corian, among other materials. In the bathroom, cold steel has been combined with the warmth of wood and ceramic furniture by the Catalano Company.

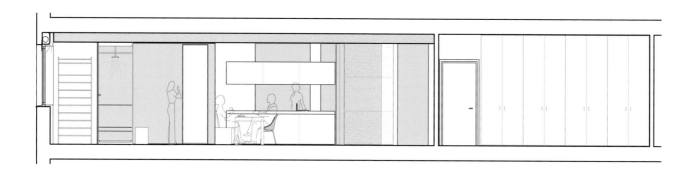

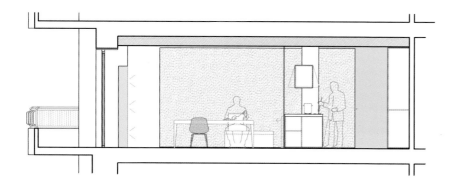

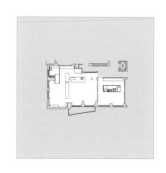

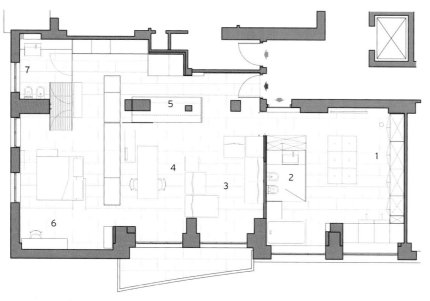

Floor plan

1. Dressing area
2. Bathroom
3. Living room
4. Dining room
5. Kitchen
6. Bedroom
7. Bathroom

▲ The bedroom area plays with a mix of shine and transparency between some of the lacquered and glass elements.

The bathroom next to the bedroom is hidden behind a red ▶
sliding door integrated in a wall of the same color.

16

ER APARTMENT
Francesc Rifé

■ Barcelona, Spain

Photos: © Gogortza & Llorella/Bisou Foto

▲ A number of cupboards were designed for the kitchen to conceal the tools needed, resulting in a more visually agreeable space.

The entrance stands out for its spectacular lighting and is a ▶ perfect introduction to a home and studio in which every point of light has been carefully designed.

▲ A smoked glass sliding door can be used to hide the bedroom when required.

The structure that contains the bedroom also includes the ▶ wardrobe which has been covered in random white slats.

This home was built along with an adjoining studio for chocolate-maker Enric Rovira, whose store is located on the ground floor. Entering from the street, the studio is on the right side while the apartment is on the left, behind a black granite staircase that begins to reveal its decorative style. Inside the apartment, the color scheme becomes palpable: white, black and oak mix repeatedly throughout the space, unifying it. The project was based on the intention of creating functional spaces that would take advantage of the limited space available while maintaining order and visual continuity. The kitchen hides all the necessities sight unseen behind its compact structure. Unlike the studio space, the living space has only one little window, which is why the area of repose and the living room are near to it and share the television and stereo equipment. With the aim of separating and hiding the different day and night areas, a smoked glass sliding door was installed. This way the bedroom is closed off into a sort of separate enclosure. The ample studio space was used by placing a table in the middle of it and display elements beside it. One of these elements is a shelving unit with different sized shelves to accommodate the different sizes of packaging used for the chocolates. The end result is a functional and compact space that has adapted fully to the needs of the owner.

▲ The sliding door that hides the bedroom also hides part of the kitchen when opened.

The structure where the bedroom has been positioned is also ▶ used as a support for the television at the foot of the bed.

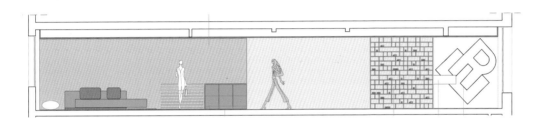

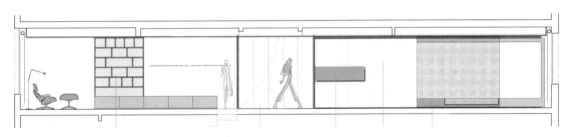

Section

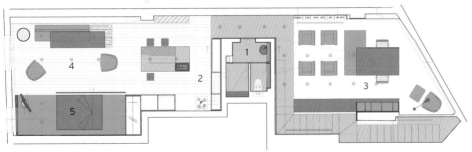

1. Bathroom
2. Kitchen
3. Studio
4. Living room
5. Bedroom

Floor plan

The relaxation area is completed with the living room right at ▲
the end of the space dedicated to the home, beside the window.

◄ One studio wall serves as a screen for projecting pictures of exquisite varieties of chocolates.

The white-lacquered DM furniture was chosen for both the ▲ living quarters and the studio space.

17

PENTHOUSE IN ANDORRA

Elisabet Faura, Gerard Veciana/Arteks

■ Andorra la Vella, Andorra

Photos: © Eugeni Pons

▲ Resin and white cement flooring was used throughout this apartment, except in particular small areas such as the bathroom and kitchen.

The wall in the hallway articulates the circulation between ▶ the day and night zones. On one side it is covered in a blackboard to make notes on.

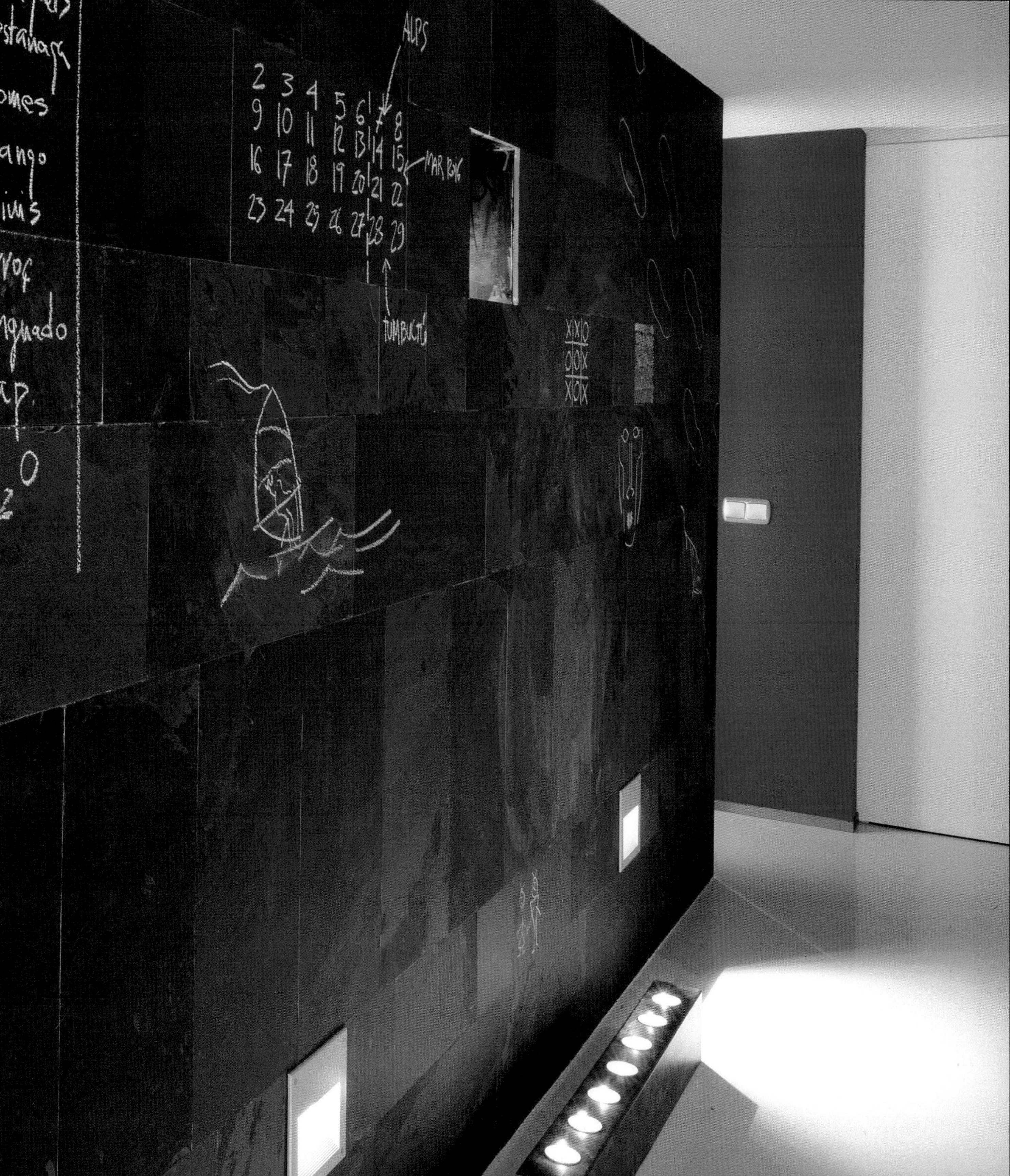
ALPS
TUMBUCTU

▲ The other side of the wall is used as a bookshelf, as this is the study and work zone.

The ceiling lists in a number of places, particularly in the ▶ kitchen and the small corner of the living room where the large window ends in a triangular shape.

Maintaining fluidity within the requirements ordained by this particular living space was one of the principal objectives behind this project. Instead of sub-dividing the surface area with traditional walls, new walls were designed with a certain thickness, texture and color. These were placed in such a way as to unite the apartment visually from one end to the other. The slate wall at the entrance determines the path of traffic between the daytime and nighttime areas of the apartment. On the side where the wall greets visitors is a place to jot down notes and reminders, where they can be seen when one leaves the apartment. On its other side is a reading area, where it becomes a book-case that hides a small office. The kitchen, dining room and living room share the same open area. Another room where sub-divisions were avoided is the master bedroom, envisioned as a suite in which the bathroom, dressing room and bedroom are compartmentalized.

In flooring the apartment, the aim was to create continuity by avoiding visible assembly points. The materials used are resin and white cement, with some exceptions. For example, the most trafficked parts of the kitchen were covered in slate while in the master bedroom, a walnut platform was used to give the area a note of warmth.

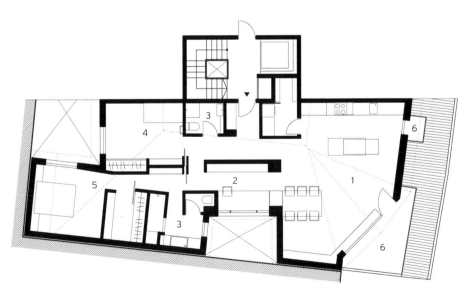

Floor plan

1. Kitchen-Dining room
2. Library
3. Bathroom
4. Bedroom
5. Master bedroom
6. Terrace

◄ The kitchen island countertop may be folded open on one side to provide a bar.

A highlight of this project is the notes of color on some of the ▲ walls and doors, such as the touch of green next to the kitchen and the red that can be seen in the background.

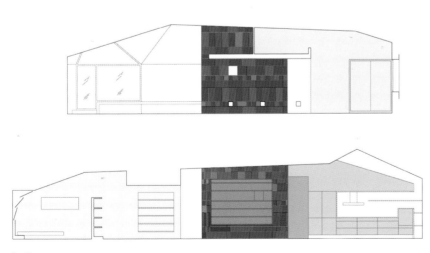

Sections

A small wall was built in the master bedroom to separate the ▲
dressing room from the bed area.

▲ The owner's affinity for mountain climbing inspired the guest room, where the beds have been raised high up.

A minimalist design reigns in the bathrooms (in this case the ▶ main bathroom), ensuring a sober, functional style.

18

JINDI BLACK-AND-WHITE CONTAINER

Mohen Design International

■ Shanghai, China

▲ The television is inserted in a panel that completely covers one wall of the living room and continues the black and white theme.

Next to the sofa, illuminated from above by a light semi-hidden in the ceiling, is the Arco lamp designed by Achille Castiglione. ▶

▲ To the left of the dining area is the corridor that connects with the bedroom, bathroom and a small indoor courtyard.

The dining room is visually connected with the living room. ▶ They are located at either end of the space used for the common areas.

The play between black and white lines of varying thickness manages a zebra effect that emphasizes this space's depth. The apartment was designed for a young executive at an international computer technology firm. With a wink towards the clarity and precision commonly identified with the technological world he inhabits, it was decided that the line itself should stand front and center in designing this space. The more subtle lines of the television stand are mixed with those made by the dining room table and the rug. Although the majority of the furniture and structures, like the sliding glass door, the tables and the lamp that hangs above one of them present smooth surfaces and straight lines, other textures, like the fine curtain and the shaggy living room rug, create a warmer, more comfortable space.

The frosted glass sliding door separates the day areas from the night. Glass, stainless steel, leather and oak are the main materials used in designing this apartment. The metallic tones and the black and white colors constitute a basic color palette that is subtly reiterated in the bathroom along with the gray colors. The living room is adorned with furniture inspired by contemporary design, like the Arco lamp and the black chair based on George Nelson's Coconut Chair.

1. Kitchen
2. Dining room
3. Living room
4. Bathroom
5. Bedroom

Floor plan

The carefully selected furniture includes a coffee table set ▲
beside the sofa, based on designs by Eileen Grey.

◀ Curtains are used throughout the property, illuminated with yellow light guides hidden in the ceiling space.

The gray tones of floor tiles and glazed tiles complement the ▲ black and white bathroom furniture.

19

DUPLEX IN LA CORUÑA
A-Cero Joaquín Torres Architects

■ La Coruña, Spain

Photos: © Alberto Bandin

▲ A height difference in the floor separates the living room from the kitchen and dining areas, shoring up the different functions of each space.

White is used on the floors and walls and contrasts with the ▶ dark tones of the furniture, such as the dining room table and kitchen island.

▲ The top floor opens onto the rest of the loft. The bedroom is visually protected by the emery-polished glass that forms the railing.

The upper floor is reached from the living room via a project- ▶ ing staircase with no riser. Above is a small chandelier that illuminates both floors.

The space now occupied by this clear and well-lit duplex was an excessively divided surface with barely any light, so the decision was made to demolish all of the partitions. The levels in the floor and the diverse pitches of the rooftop allow for a differentiation to be made between each area while still enjoying a visual communication between them. Despite the elimination of some of the walls, all of the storage areas were kept, including the closet at the entrance, the pantry and dish cabinets, as well as the space reserved for the washer and cleaning supplies.

The finishes reinforce the notion of austerity that served as a basis for the design of this penthouse duplex. This is why all of the walls, floors and ceilings are white, except for the bathroom walls, which are made of glass in order to achieve a waterproof surface.

The home is divided into two floors. On the bottom floor are the kitchen, dining room, courtesy bathroom and the living room; this last one is separated from the rest by a subtle lift at floor level. By going up the riser-less hanging stairs, under which was laid a decorative ledge, the bedroom and main bathroom can be found, each with their own lighting system capable of creating outstanding atmospheres. All of the furniture has been exclusively designed for this project, from the picture frames to the chairs. One of the biggest challenges was the kitchen closet, since it had to hold all of the appliances.

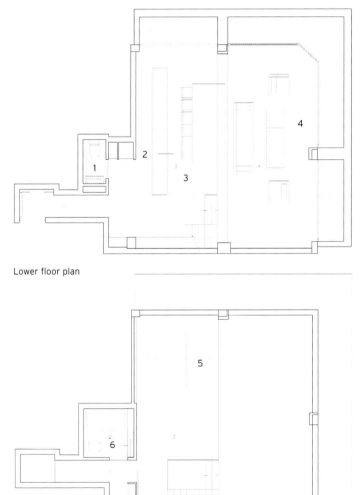

Lower floor plan

Upper floor plan

1. Bathroom
2. Kitchen
3. Dining room
4. Living room
5. Bedroom
6. Bathroom

The bedroom is an example of austerity and simplicity, with ▲ a futon bed and glass opening that peaks into the living room.

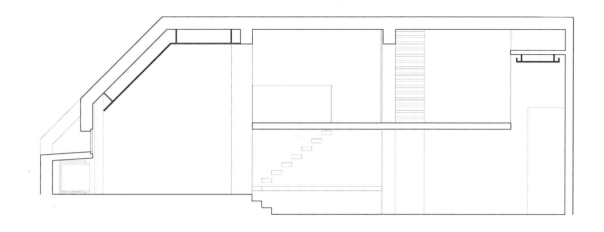

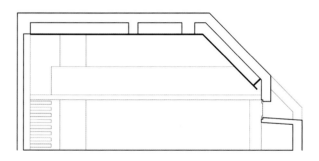

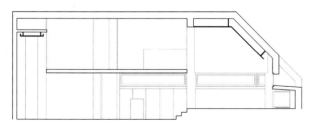

Sections

20

FANLING CENTER
PTang Studio

■ Hong Kong, China

Photos: © Philip Tang

▲ One of the most characteristic elements of this property is found in the living room: a green wall, which becomes a focal point.

The entry is visually connected with the study, located at the ▶ other end. To the right are the kitchen, dining room and bathroom, while the living room is on the left.

▲ The living room looks out onto the mountains close to the New Territories residential neighborhood of Hong Kong where the apartment is located.

Of particular note in the living room are the wall, sofa and ▶ the coffee table. The other elements are simple and minimalist and go practically unnoticed.

This apartment is situated in a quiet residential neighborhood in New Territories, in Hong Kong. Its minimalist aesthetic is reinforced by the use of a specific color palette that is repeated throughout each room. The color white is the true protagonist here, seconded by apple green, wood tones and red brushstrokes that create a fresh and spring-like ambience. Behind the hall is the kitchen, painted a spotless white. Beyond this can be found the main area, where the dining room and living room are located. The lines are pure in the furniture that decorates these rooms and are either white or gray or made of wood. The green wall behind the sofa lends a discordant note. Also, the bedroom has been designed to include a small study, thus taking advantage of the fact that there are two more sources of natural light. The bathroom is the only room to break the chromatic harmony and the apartment's general aesthetic; it's paved and dressed with black tile, though the furniture remains white in color. The apartment suggests a clean space, playing with a linear minimalism that is complemented by colorful notes in decorative elements like frames and accessories that lend a dose of energy.

▲ White is the true protagonist of this project, where a relaxed, harmonious ambience is achieved with light-toned wood.

The kitchen is located off the entrance, on the right-hand ▶ side. It was painted bright white to make it look bigger.

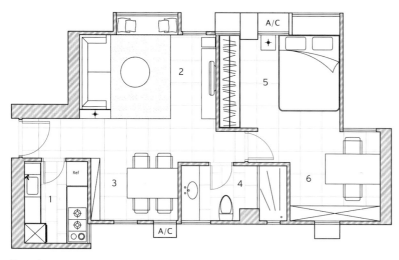

1. Kitchen
2. Living room
3. Dining room
4. Bathroom
5. Bedroom
6. Study

Floor plan

◄ The bathroom is the counterpoint to the rest of the project, achieving a personal air of elegance with the black tiles.

All the elements that finish the bathroom were chosen in ▲ white, to contrast with the black that predominates.

◄ A small bend in the bedroom was used to make a study with a desk and cupboards behind it.

Timber, red and green are repeated in the bedroom, such as ▲ in the unusual red cylindrical lamp at the foot of the bed.

21

FOR YOUR EYES ONLY
Christian Schuster

■ Geseke, Germany

▲ The main element is undoubtedly the large circular opening above the sofa, which becomes the center of attention and was the focal point of the project.

From the entrance, a curved path leads to the living room, ▶ decorated in a minimalist fashion, featuring a large red rug with the coffee table on top.

▲ When the mechanism of this unusual round window is fully opened, it reveals the red leather frame that surrounds it.

The living room television module has a white lacquered ▶ front and is divided in two by a backlit strip of glass.

Given the challenge of converting a multifunctional space into a small apartment, architect Christian Schuster designed a property that pays tribute to James Bond. A number of elements were fitted with original mechanisms reminiscent of Bond, as well as a retro look also characteristic of the 007 films. All the daytime areas were integrated into a single zone and unified in a free space with no separations. The large picture window that runs along one wall in this unified area lights a large part of the home. The union between the living room and bedroom is achieved with an innovative solution: the wall that separates the two spaces has been fitted with a circular opening with an iris that is opened and closed by remote control, adding to the futuristic look of the apartment. When fully open, the iris reveals a red leather frame and can be converted into an improvised chair.

The module containing the different kitchen elements has a red lacquer finish. This color is a leitmotif in the apartment's décor and is repeated in various elements in each zone. The kitchen table includes another mechanism, this time simple and manual but just as functional as the one that separates the living room from the bedroom. It is a low wall on which the timber tabletop lies. The tabletop can easily slide across and become either the kitchen table or another element of the living room. The floor throughout the home is stained a very subtle pink color that perfectly matches the white and timber, as well as the red.

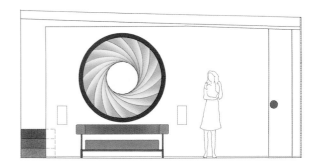
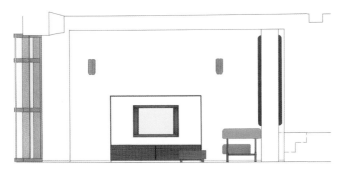
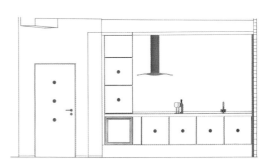

Interior elevations

1. Kitchen
2. Dining room
3. Living room
4. Bedroom
5. Bathroom

Floor plan

The plan shows how most of the apartment's surface area has been used for the day zones, which share the same space.

The dining room or kitchen chairs, positioned in one place or the other depending on which way the tabletop slides out, are the Tulip model from designer Eero Saarinen.

▲ The wall next to the kitchen is covered in gray lacquered glass, differentiating this space within the common area.

In the bathroom next to the bedroom, the solid zebrano- ▶ wood washbasin with a red lacquered frame is of particular note.

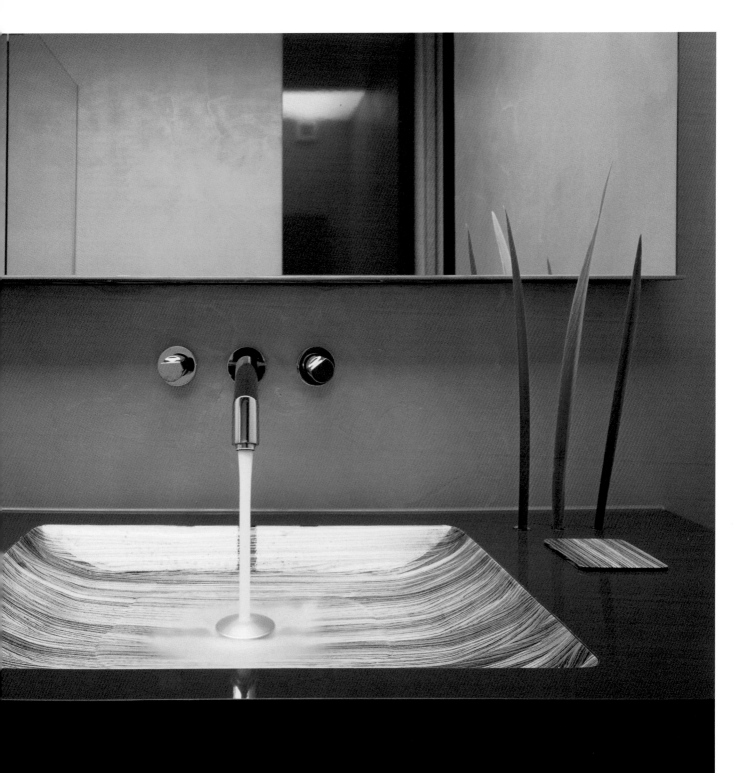

▲ In the bedroom, the bed is right underneath the circular opening made in the wall that separates this room from the living room.

22

APARTMENT IN ATTIC

■ Brussels, Belgium

Photos: © Vercruysse & Dujardin/Owi.bz

▲ A small staircase that made it possible to maximize the space on the ground floor was built to reach the bedroom.

The dining room, with a table that opens at one end, features ▶ DSR chairs in white plastic and steel, designed by Charles and Ray Eames.

▲ The tabletop can also open and includes an empty space for storing the flatware. The kitchen module houses the rest of the cupboards.

The bathroom is reached via the kitchen and is right underneath the space given over to the bedroom on the upper floor. ▶

This small, futuristic-style apartment was remodeled and designed as a temporary residence. It involved a provisional solution while much more expensive and lengthy work was being done to the rest of the house, which would become the owners' permanent home. This temporary nature was the perfect excuse to experiment with a bold and daring design that would simplify the necessary elements as much as possible because of the small space available. The inspiration for this project clearly comes from the design and futuristic films that proliferated throughout the 1960s and 1970s. Its rounded, organic forms are a very useful tool in small spaces like this.

One of the main changes involved the design of a structure that runs around the small living room, kitchen and bathroom. It includes various spaces and holes in which the stove and oven were positioned, the kitchen cupboards arranged and the bathroom inserted, reached via a door reminiscent of one on a space ship. The dining table provides another clever space-saving solution, as inside it there is a small empty space for storing the microwave oven. The top floor houses the bedroom and a study, where the desk is the prolongation of the brown surface that surrounds the sink on the floor below.

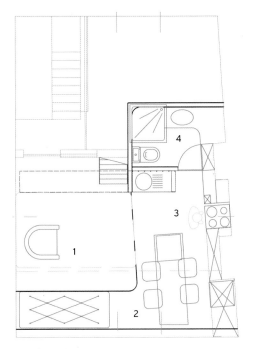

Lower floor plan

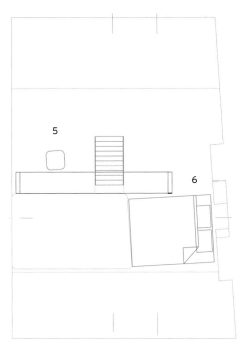

Upper floor plan

1. Living room
2. Dining room
3. Kitchen
4. Bathroom
5. Study
6. Bedroom

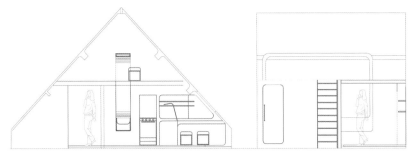

Sections

◀ These sections correspond to the ones shown on the plans. They demonstrate how the sink structure rises to the top floor and forms the desk.

A light underneath the structure below the dining room and ▲ kitchen highlights the futuristic look of the property.

▲ A simple mattress can be used in the improvised living room.
An original bar has been designed for the space behind it.

The upper level is open to the lower one, meaning the light ▶
that comes in the study window also illuminates the rest of
the apartment.

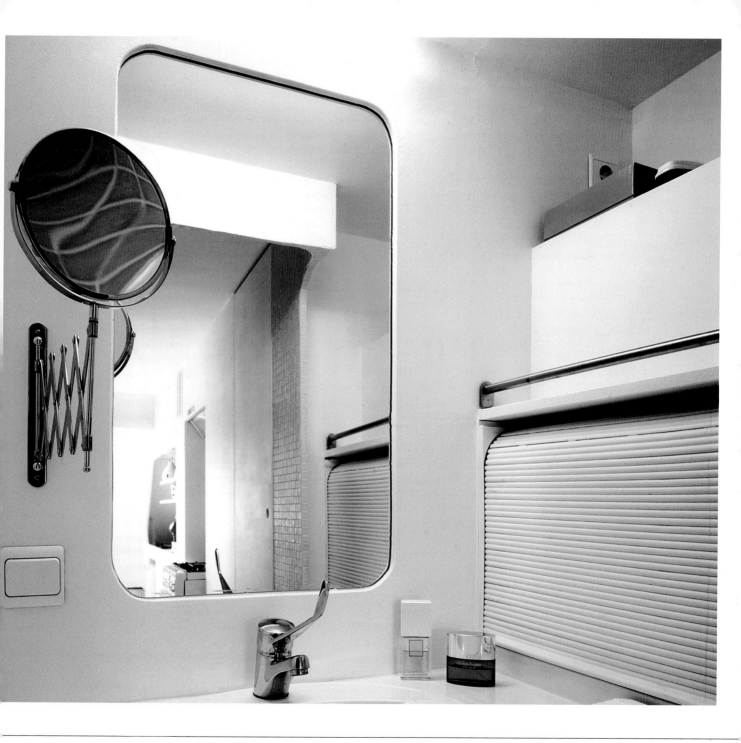

◀ The desk in the study runs from one end to the other, leaving a space big enough for the futon-style bed.

The small bathroom includes a shower tray, a toilet and a ▲ washbasin. It is pure white and has few elements.

23

APARTMENT IN ROME

Filippo Bombace

■ Rome, Italy

Photos: © Luigi Filetici

▲ One of the most colorful elements in the living room is the Mussi sofa, upholstered with Kvadrat fabric, the colors of which exactly match those of the mural on the wall.

The curtain frames visually separate the entrance from the ▶ living room. Here the privacy of the property has been preserved from the main door while also creating a corridor to the kitchen.

▲ The kitchen stands out for its simplicity, fitted with just one pearl gray and black lacquered bench with a steel surface. It includes a small breakfast bar.

The wall of the corridor that leads to the kitchen is also a ▶ pantry. It even includes the fridge, representing a clever solution to the problem of the lack of space.

From the windows of this apartment you can enjoy one of the world's most famous settings - the Roman Colosseum. This privileged view was the source of inspiration for the architect Filippo Bombace when remodeling the property, as well as the family's express desire to maintain a traditional distribution. The choice and application of colors became the starting points for the project. Each tone is based on an association with nearby elements, such as the grayish tones inspired by the color of the Roman stones, the travertine beige and the bishop's purple. These colors are particularly reflected in the fabric of the sofa and the large living room mural which the architect designed. Next to it is the New Concepts bookshelf by Acergbis, behind which is concealed a blue fluorescent light.

The kitchen is open-plan and communicates directly with the living room. It is reached via a corridor that has two functions, as it contains cupboards and a refrigerator, making it into a type of storeroom. The apartment has two bathrooms which are accessed from the corridor and where the architect opted for sliding doors to make the most of the space. In front is the main bedroom, where, as well as the bed, a small mezzanine level has been designed to fit a study, making it into an improvised vantage point for the Colosseum. The color details are repeated throughout the property, both in the bathrooms (one in shades of yellow and the other in lilac), and the other bedrooms.

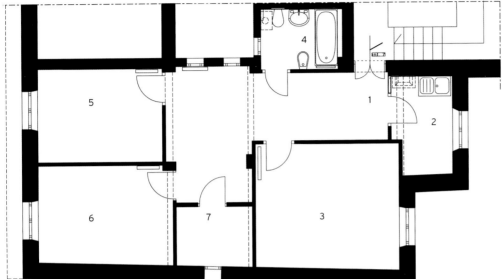

Existing floor plan

1. Entrance Hall
2. Kitchen
3. Living room
4. Bathroom
5. Bedroom 1
6. Bedroom 2
7. Room

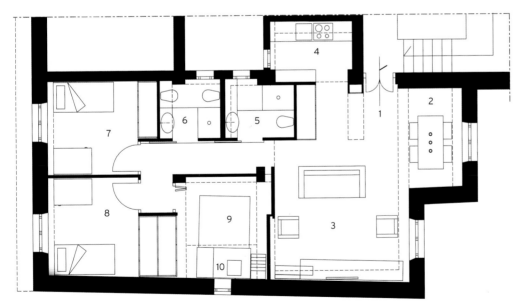

New floor plan

1. Entrance Hall
2. Dining room
3. Living room
4. Kitchen
5. Bathroom 1
6. Bathroom 2
7. Bedroom 1
8. Bedroom 2
9. Master Bedroom
10. Studio

The plain and simple bathroom is covered in Black Ardesia ▲
tessera glass by Ariostea, and the tap is the Rettangolo model from Gessi.

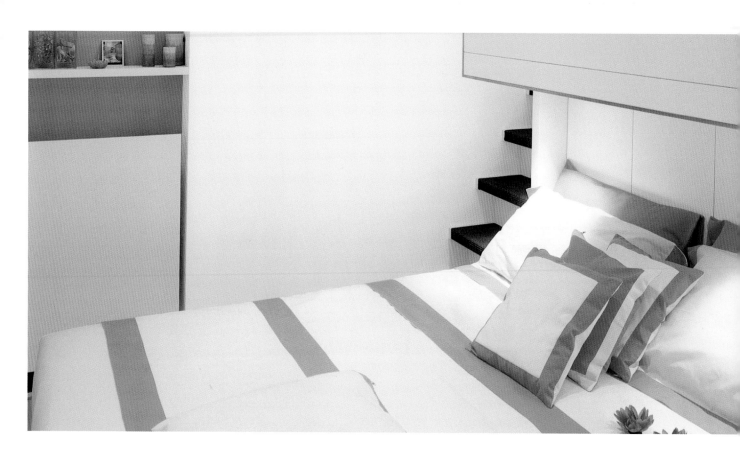

Section

◄ The stairs at the side of the bed lead to the mezzanine level located immediately above, where the small study is found.

This double-height ceiling in the study affords views over the ▲ Roman Colosseum through the small window.

24

MIAMI PIED-À-TERRE

Pablo Uribe/Studio Uribe

■ Miami, USA

Photos: © Claudia Uribe

▲ The main materials used in this apartment are the concrete that completely covers the floor and the aluminum of the windows.

The white walls and lack of partitions maximize the light in ▶ the whole of the apartment.

▲ The bedroom is located next to one of the windows at the opposite end of the access to the home, where it is visually concealed.

The simple kitchen is positioned in the entrance, opposite ▶ the dining room table and set against the wall in front of the bathroom.

This apartment was designed for a couple that already owned a place in Miami, though it wasn't on the beach. In other words, this project was about a space that would be used sporadically while being functional and fully integrated. The lack of actual walls meant the project started off as a clean canvas. The principal elements used are polished cement on the floors, aluminum for the window frames and white color on the walls. The kitchen was built at the entrance to the loft, taking advantage of the vestibule as a place to cook, right across from the round dining room table. This same area holds the kitchen, dining room, living room and the corner where the desk is. Just behind it is a balcony that, while small, is perhaps the most used room in the home. Because of this, a comfortable bench was installed to better enjoy the sea breeze while resting atop a comfy set of cushions.

Just in front of the living room is the bedroom. Each shares the same visual and actual space, so that the couch can be seen from the bed and vice versa, though they are quite far apart. Next to the bedroom and behind a curtain is the dressing room, located on the way to the bathroom. The ceiling is slightly lower in these last two areas, lending a subtle sensation of privacy without resorting to doors or other divisive elements. This way, from the shower, a good part of the loft can be seen, not to mention the exterior, which is visible through the windows.

◀ The areas of repose, the living room and bedroom, face each other without need for separating elements.

White and blue create an idyllic atmosphere on this small ▲ balcony, where long hours can be spent looking at the palm trees and the ocean that laps the shores of Miami.

▲ The dressing room and bathroom are to the left of the bedroom, in what is practically an open space.

▲ The lack of furniture and other accessories makes the bathroom a simple and minimalist space.

The shower, located on the other side of the wall from the ▶ kitchen, is completely open to the bedroom.

25

GASTOWN LOFT
Splyce Design

■ Vancouver, Canada

Photos: © Michael Bolan

▲ Transferring the office to the upstairs extension made it possible to use the space opposite the kitchen to house the dining room table.

The breakfast bar and upstairs extension emphasize the ▶ visual limits of the kitchen, even though it is open to the rest of the loft.

◄ Some design pieces really stand out, such as the Arne Jacob-sen Ant chairs in the dining room and the LCW model by Charles and Ray Eames next to the breakfast bar.

The visual union between the two floors is shored up by ► openings in the floor of the new office.

The existing loft had an undefined and impersonal design in which the domestic spaces had the standard and original fittings from when the loft was first built. One of the main premises the project started from was to define each functional space but maintain a consistency and union between them. The kitchen became the principal focus of the redesign work, as it defines and is also defined by the adjacent spaces.

In order to accommodate a space for the dining room beside the kitchen, an extension of the upper floor was designed to house the office, which used to occupy the place where the dining room table now is. This upstairs extension also visually boosted the limits of the kitchen, as it is separated from the living room via a bar used as a work surface and table. The refrigerator is hidden behind a sliding door next to the closet opposite the bathroom. This made it possible to create two accesses to the bathroom, from the corridor and from the kitchen, via an opaque sliding door with a translucent glass strip. The white lacquered kitchen cupboards mix with the timber, follow the line of the white walls and shore up the feeling of spaciousness and light. Upstairs, timber comes to the fore, as seen in the module that separates the bedroom from the office.

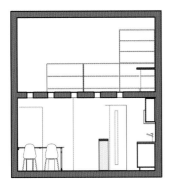

North elevation

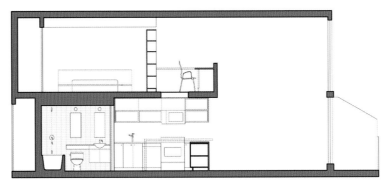

West elevation

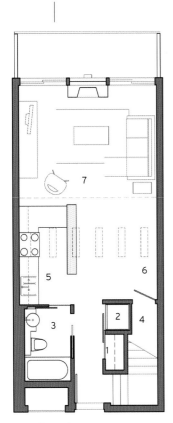

Lower floor plan

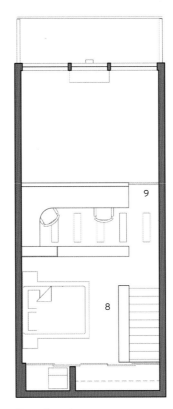

Upper floor plan

1. Wardrobe
2. Refrigerator alcove
3. Bathroom
4. Storage
5. Kitchen
6. Dining room
7. Living room
8. Bedroom
9. Office

The space the refrigerator used to be in was used to position ▲
a sliding door that permits access to the bathroom from the
kitchen.

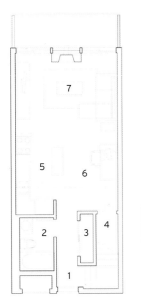

Existing floor plan
Lower

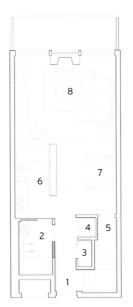

New floor plan
Lower

◀ These plans show the redesign work done in the kitchen. To put the dining room in the space opposite, the office was moved upstairs.

Existing floor plan
1. Hall
2. Bathroom
3. Closet
4. Storage
5. Kitchen
6. Studio
7. Living room

New floor plan
1. Hall
2. Bathroom
3. Closet
4. Refrigerator
5. Storage
6. Kitchen
7. Dining room
8. Living room

◀ The upstairs extension hangs over the rest of the loft and enables the natural light to reach all the rooms.

The bedroom has a sober and simple design. A timber struc- ▲ ture acts as a separator with respect to the office, with a hole for the light to penetrate.

26

SPACE OF FEMININITY

Mohen Design International

■ Shanghai, China

Photos: © Mohen Design International

▲ The round, colored shapes of the living room furniture, like the sofa, pouffe and armchair, embody the property's fresh, fun look.

An interaction exists between the living room and the ▶ kitchen, reinforced by the design of a large arch.

▲ A number of empty spaces have been made in the walls for use as shelves or decorative elements like the circumferences.

Part of the lighting of this apartment is hidden in the ceiling ▶ space and the openings made in the walls.

The use of curved elements and surfaces, as well as the wide color range chosen, makes this apartment for a young, single woman a unique place to be surrounded by femininity. The doors have been converted into huge openings surrounded by a round, maroon painted frame. This way, enclosures are avoided and, as is the case with the least private spaces, the living room and kitchen, these openings are made even bigger to better unite both areas. The walls have been painted a light salmon color so that the rest of the decorative elements really stand out. In the living room, all attention is drawn to the sofa, love seat and the brightly colored pouffe, all upholstered in suede. A glossy maroon hollow has been made to serve as a bookcase in one of the walls; behind the sofa a mirror has been placed below the point of light. The details are some of this project's more personal elements; like the reliefs, with their concentric circles of varying depth or the orange methacrylate doors on some of the kitchen cabinets. The walls and floor of the bathroom have been entirely decorated with pieces that form a mosaic of red and maroon tonality to create a bright and energetic space. In the bedroom, the wall at the head of the bed forms a curve at the top of the ceiling, repeating once again the stamps of identity that are a part of this apartment, as in the case of the circumferences and the colorful lines also visible in this location.

The colored wall and fun egg-shaped armchairs that deco- ▲
rate the hall are the perfect prelude to the apartment's strik-
ing décor.

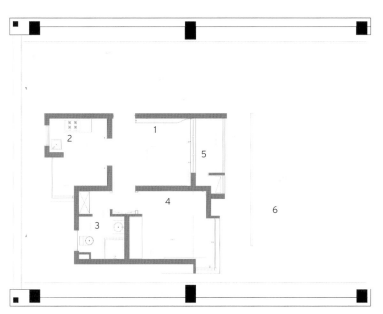

Floor plan

1. Living room
2. Kitchen
3. Bathroom
4. Bedroom
5. Terrace
6. Hallway

All sorts of elements are used as a palette to fill the bedroom ▲ with color and patterns. The curved shapes are repeated again, as can be seen on the ceiling.

The explosion of color is even more apparent in the bath- ▶
room, for which an eye-catching mosaic was chosen.

27

APARTMENT IN MADRID

Rocío Fueyo Casado

■ Madrid, Spain

Photos: © Jordi Miralles

▲ During the remodeling, the structure of columns and beams was uncovered, exposing the insides of the building and making the space look bigger.

Two staircases were built to reach the top floor, which was ▶ gained from the existing space by knocking down partition walls and ceilings. Each staircase leads to one of the two separate upstairs areas.

◆ The plastic paint on the beams and washable paint on the walls, both in white, reflect maximum natural light. A lacquer was used for the orange wall.

The partition walls are made from plasterboard, except in ▶ the bathroom which is brick. The floor in the living and dressing rooms is light-colored timber.

The remodeling of this apartment located in the Malasaña area of central Madrid was carried out optimizing resources and minimizing costs. The duplex is situated in an old neighborhood formed of small homes reached by passageways or corridors and laid out around an interior courtyard. The house was in a dreadful state. In barely 430 square feet, the ground floor (the only floor prior to the remodeling work) consisted of a living room, two bedrooms, a kitchen with a toilet and just three windows. The first step was to knock down all the walls and ceilings and only conserve the structure of columns and beams that held up the ceiling. Leaving the partition walls uncovered made it possible to put in more windows, as there had only been three in the whole of the property.

The enlargement meant the space could be redistributed to obtain two floors. The bottom floor now houses the living room, a bathroom, the kitchen and a dressing room. Upstairs, which has two separate accesses, there are a bedroom and study in the biggest area and a small guest bedroom in the other space. The two zones look down over the bottom floor. To reach them, two staircases were built: one inspired by the Jacques Tati film Mon Oncle, formed of a projecting iron structure with no rail; the other made of fine pieces of metal screwed into the wall. The ground-floor ceilings start at a height of 8.6 feet and reach 18 feet in the areas with a double height. The upper floor ceiling has a maximum height of just under six feet and is slightly more than two feet at its lowest point.

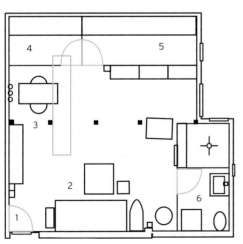

Lower floor plan

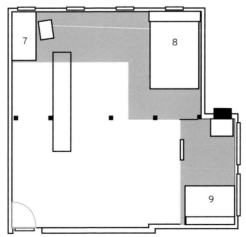

Upper floor plan

1. Entrance
2. Living room
3. Dining room
4. Dressing room
5. Kitchen
6. Bathroom
7. Study
8. Bedroom
9. Guest bedroom

◀ The dining area, with a small table, is located next to the main staircase and uses the bend formed together with the column.

To minimize costs, the hydraulic tiles on the kitchen floor ▲ were rescued from the living room of the old home.

▲ The vaulted bedroom ceiling is just over two feet high at its lowest point. On the other side of the stairwell is the small study.

Simple lines and the color white are used in the bathroom, ▶ with fun touches of bright colors.

28

GRAMERCY PARK APARTMENT

Page Goolrick

■ New York, USA

▲ The area where the apartment's bedroom used to be is now
a dining room that joins the living room.

White walls and light colors like the beige rug, which contrast ▶
with the wenge wood and dark brown, create an elegant and
welcoming space.

▲ Basic functional pieces combining white and steel were positioned in the narrow, elongated small space used for the kitchen.

The new distribution of the property's spaces puts the ▶ kitchen next to the bedroom, a strange choice fixed with the use of sliding panels to define each zone.

Sometimes, a small space will require big ideas in order to take full advantage of all its possibilities. The remodeling of this loft, originally devoid of actual rooms, resulted in a great redistribution effort. Aside from designing a bedroom, solutions were sought for maximizing the use of natural light in the main rooms and achieving an agreeable *pied-à-terre*. The first step was to change the location of the kitchen, which had windows that faced the exterior. By rotating it ninety degrees, the kitchen was placed next to the bathroom and became open to the rest of the apartment while remaining sheltered in one of the nooks and crannies found on the premises. Now, the space previously occupied by the kitchen is reserved for the bedroom, making use of natural light thanks to the old kitchen

window. It was also decided that the bedroom be surrounded by opaque paneling on the side that connects with the living room, while the side that connects with the kitchen has been surrounded by translucent panels. This allows for the unification of private areas with communal ones or, when desired, for their separation.

Every space has been used to full advantage in this project's design and all materials used were carefully chosen to endow the space with maximum flexibility. The use of lighter tones lends the apartment a greater sense of spaciousness. The furniture inside adheres to a minimalist approach predominated by white and beige, as well as being combined with brown-colored pieces that complement the decoration and achieve a chromatic counterpoint.

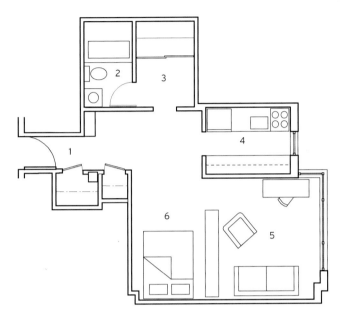

Existing floor plan

1. Hall
2. Bathroom
3. Dressing area
4. Kitchen
5. Living room
6. Bedroom

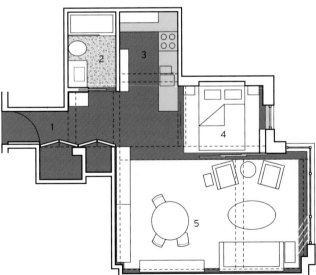

New floor plan

1. Hall
2. Bathroom
3. Kitchen
4. Bedroom
5. Living room-dining room

◀ These plans show the remodeling work carried out on the property. The bedroom occupies the space where the kitchen used to be, which is now next to the bathroom.

To make the most use of natural light, translucent panels ▲ were used for the separation of bedroom and kitchen.

▲ This loft can be converted into a completely open space by drawing back the panels around the bedroom.

To make the small bathroom feel as roomy as possible, the ▶ door was replaced with a sliding door and the walls and furniture were kept light in tone.

A-Cero Joaquín Torres Architects
Parque Empresarial La Finca
Paseo Club Deportivo nº 1, bloque A
28223 Pozuelo de Alarcón, Madrid, Spain
T/F: +34 91 799 79 84
a-cero@a-cero.com
www.a-cero.com
Duplex in La Coruña
Photos: © Alberto Bandin

Bruno Vanbesien
Nieuwland 43
1000 Brussels, Belgium
T/F: +32 2 787 00 95
mail@brunovanbesien.be
www.brunovanbesien.be
Duplex in Brussels
Photos: © Hendikx Diane/Owi.bz

Christian Schuster
Siemensstrasse 3
59590 Geseke, Germany
T: +49 2942 9724 19
F: +49 2942 9724 20
info@christianschuster.com
www.christianschuster.com
For Your Eyes Only
Photos: © Ludger Paffrath

CJ Studio
Floor 6, nº 54, Lane 260 Kwang Fu South Road
Taipei, Taiwan
T: +886 2773 8366
F: +886 2773 8365
cj@shi-chieh-lu.com
www.shi-chieh-lu.com
Chen Residence
Photos: © CJ Studio

DAP Studio
Via G. B. Brocchi 7/A
20131 Milan, Italy
T: +39 02 70631511
F: +39 02 2361496
dap@newmedia.it
www.dapstudio.com
Piazza Biancamano Apartment
Photos: © Andrea Martiradonna

Dick van Gameren Architecten
(deelnemer aan de architectengroep BV)
Barenstszplein 7
1013 NJ Amsterdam, The Netherlands
T: +31 020 530 4850
F: +31 020 530 4860
info@vangameren.com
www.dickvangameren.com
Duplex in Drufaystraat
Photos: © Luuk Kramer

Elisabet Faura, Gerard Veciana/Arteks
L'Aigüeta 12, 1º
AD500 Andorra la Vella, Andorra
T: +376 823 202
F: +376 823 272
info@arteks.ad
www.arteks.ad
Penthouse in Andorra
Photos: © Eugeni Pons

Filippo Bombace
Via Monte Tomatico 1
00141 Rome, Italy
T: +39 06 8689 8266
F: +39 06 8689 8529
info@ filippobombace.com
www.filippobombace.com
Apartment in Rome
Photos: © Luigi Filetici

Flora de Gastines & Anne Geistdoerfer/Double G
50 rue de Sévigné
75003 Paris, France
T: +39 1 42 78 17 56
flora@doubleg.fr
www.doubleg.fr
Apartment in Paris
Photos: © André Thoraval

Francesc Rifé
Escoles Pies 25, baixos
08017 Barcelona, Spain
T: +34 93 414 12 88
f@rife-design.com
www.rife-design.com
ER Apartment
Photos: © Gogortza&Llorella/Bisou Foto

Gavin Harris, Henrietta Reed/Mackay & Partners LLP
63 Gee Street
London EC1V 3RS, United Kingdom
T: +44 20 7608 1177
F: +44 20 7168 8000
g.harris@mackayandpartners.co.uk
www.mackayandpartners.co.uk
Apartment H
Photos: © Niall Clutton

Geneviève Marginet
Apartment in Attic
Photos: © Vercruysee & Dujardin/Owi.bz

Kim Utzon Arkitekter
Nordre Tolbod 23
DK-1259 Copenhagen, Denmark
T: +45 3393 4334
info@kimutzon.dk
www.utzon-arkitekter.dk
Pier 24 Copenhagen
Photos: © Carlos Cezanne

Kyu Sung Woo Architects
488 Green Street
Cambridge, MA 02139, USA
T: +1 617 657 0128
F: +1 617 547 9675
kswa@kswa.com
www.kswa.com
Interlocking Puzzle Loft
Photos: © Adam Friedberg

Leone Design Studio
55 Washington Street 253B, Brooklyn
New York, NY 11201, USA
T: +1 718 243 9088
F: +1 718 243 0454
info@leonedesignstudio.com
www.leonedesignstudio.com
West 87th Street Apartment
Photos: © Mikiko Kikuyama

Mohen Design International
Nº 18, Alley 396, Wulumuqi S. Rd.
200031 Shanghai, China
T: +86 21 64370910
F: +86 21 64317125
mohen@mohen-design.com
www.mohen-design.com
Jindi Black-and-White Container
Metropolitan Chic
Space of Feminity
Photos: © Mohen Design International

nArchitects
68 Jay Street 317, Brooklyn
New York, NY 11201, USA
T: +1 718 260 0845
F: +1 718 260 0847
www.narchitects.com
Ply Loft
Photos: © Frank Oudeman

Pablo Fernández Lorenzo & Pablo Redondo Díez
San Marcos 3
28004 Madrid, Spain
T: +34 91 521 95 82
pablofl@coam.es
It's Fab to Have my Own Pad
Photos: © Pablo Fernández Lorenzo

Pablo Uribe/Studio Uribe
1225 Lenox Avenue
Miami Beach, FL 22139, USA
T: +1 305 695 1415
design@studiouribe.com
www.studiouribe.com
Miami Pied-à-terre
Photos: © Claudia Uribe

Page Goolrick Architect PC
20 West 22 Street
New York, NY 10010, USA
T: +1 212 219 3666
F: +1 212 414 5768
info@goolrick.com
www.goolrick.com
Gramercy Park Apartment
Photos: © John M. Hall

Poponcini & Lootens Architecten Bvba
Tavernierkaai 2 bus 28
2000 Antwerpen, Brussels
T: +32 3 225 18 84
F: +32 3 233 22 67
info@polo-architects.be
www.polo-architects.be
Small Space
Photos: © Sarah Blee/Owi.bz

PTang Studio Ltd
Rm 603-604, Harry Industrial Building
49-51 Au Pui Wan Street, Sha Tin
New Territories, Hong Kong
T: +852 2669 1577
F: +852 2669 3577
office@ptangstudio.com
www.ptangstudio.com
Fanling Center
Photos: © Philip Tang
La Rossa
Photos: © Ulso Tsang

Rocío Fueyo Casado
Apartment in Madrid
Photos: © Jordi Miralles

Splyce Design/Build Inc
405-289 Alexander Street
Vancouver BC V6A 4H6, Canada
T: +1 604 765 0592
F: +1 604 408 0592
info@splyce.ca
www.splyce.ca
Gastown Loft
Photos: © Michael Boland

The Lawrence Group Architects Inc
307 West 38th Street, suite 1618
New York, NY 10018, USA
T: +1 212 764 2424
F: +1 212 354 6909
info@thelawrencegroup.com
www.thelawrencegroup.com
Florence Residence
Photos: © Frank Oudeman